Weird and Amazing Places
in the
Natural World

By TJ Rob

Weird and Amazing Places in the NATURAL World
By TJ Rob

Wonders of the World — Volume 2

Copyright Text TJ Rob, 2016
All rights reserved. No part of the book may be reproduced in any form without permission in writing from the author. Reviewers may quote brief passages in review.
ISBN 978-1-988695-24-2

Disclaimer:
No part of this book may be reproduced in any form or by any means, mechanical or electronic, including photocopying or recording, or by an information storage and retrieval system, or transmitted by email without permission in writing from the publisher. This book is for entertainment purposes only. The views expressed are those of author alone.

Published by:
TJ Rob
Suite 609
440-10816 Macleod Trail SE
Calgary, AB T2J 5N8 www.TJRob.com

Photo Credits: Images used under license from Shutterstock.com, Flickr.com, Wikimedia Commons, Creative Commons and Public Domain:

Cover page, photo.ua/Shutterstock.com; Cover page, Olimpiu Pop/Shutterstock.com; pg. 1, Travis Wise/Flickr.com; pg. 4, Joanna Penn/Flickr.com; pg. 5, Sahajesh Patel/Flickr.com; pg. 5, Виктор В CC BY-SA 3.0/Wkimedia Commons; pg. 6, llee_wu/Flickr.com; pg. 7, llee_wu/Flickr.com; pg. 7, Rei-artur CC BY-SA 3.0/Wikimedia Commons; pg. 8, U.S. Geological Survey (USGS)/Public Domain; pg. 9, Mr Minton/Flickr.com; pg. 10, Anouchka Unel/Wikimedia Commons; pg. 11, Luigi Chiesa/Public Domain; pg. 11, Luca Galuzzi CC BY-SA 2.5/Wkimedia Commons; pg. 12, Brad Coy/Flickr.com; pg. 12, TUBS CC BY-SA 3.0/Wkimedia Commons; pg. 13, Brad Coy/Flickr.com; pg. 14, Darren J. Bradley/Shutterstock.com; pg. 15, photo.ua/Shutterstock.com; pg. 16, Mark Bergman/Public Domain; pg. 17, Olimpiu Pop/Shutterstock.com; pg. 19, TUBS CC BY-SA 3.0/Wikimedia Commons; pg. 18, William Warby CC BY 2.0/Wikimedia Commons; pg. 19, Chris Murphy/Flickr.com; pg. 19, Demetrius John Kessy CC BY 2.0/Wikimedia Commons; pg. 19, Vincenzo Gianferrari Pini CC BY-SA 2.5/Wkimedia Commons; pg. 20, FarbenfroheWunderwelt/Flickr.com; pg. 20, Виктор В CC BY-SA 3.0/Wkimedia Commons; pg. 21, Fascinating Universe CC BY-SA 3.0/Wkimedia Commons; pg. 22, J Zapell/Public Domain; pg. 23, Mark Muir/Wikimedia Commons; pg. 24, Curioso/Shutterstock.com; pg. 25, Rodrigo Soldon/Flickr.com; pg. 25, Yutaka Fujii/Flickr.com; pg. 26, John Vetterli/Flickr.com; pg. 27, Ryan Cadby/Flickr.com; pg. 28, Grand Canyon National Park/Flickr.com; pg. 29, Moyan Brenn/Flickr.com; pg. 30, Chmee2 CC BY 3.0/Wikimedia Commons; pg. 31, missfitz CC BY 2.0/Wikimedia Commons; pg. 31, Edwin Poon/Flickr.com; pg. 32, By Uryah CC BY-SA 3.0/Wikimedia Commons; pg. 33, 663highland CC-BY-SA-3.0/Creative Commons

TABLE OF CONTENTS

	Page
Uluru - Australia's Giant Rock	4
Ha Long Bay - Where the Dragon Descends into the Sea	6
The Great Blue Hole - Belize	8
The Salar de Uyuni - A Sea of Salt	10
The Blue Grotto - Capri	12
Arches National Park - Utah, USA	14
The Matterhorn - Switzerland and Italy	16
Ngorongoro Crater - Tanzania, Africa	18
The Great Barrier Reef - Australia	20
Pando - The Trembling Giant - Utah, USA	22
Iguazu Falls - Brazil, South America	24
The Grand Canyon - Arizona, USA	26
The Giant's Causeway - Northern Ireland	30
Yuki-no-Otani Snow Canyon, Honshu, Japan	32
Please leave a review and Other EXCITING books by TJ Rob	34

ULURU
Australia's GIANT ROCK

Uluru is also known as Ayers Rock. It was named in 1873 after Sir Henry Ayers, the 8th Premier of South Australia.

Uluru is the Aboriginal and official name.

The rock was created over 600 million years ago, and the Aborigines have been in the area for the last 10,000 years.

It originally sat at the bottom of a sea, but today stands 1,141 feet (348m) above the ground. It also extends more than 1.5 miles (2.5km) beneath the surface.

Uluru is made of sandstone. It gets its orange-red color from the rock's high iron content.

Uluru is 2,831 feet (863 meters) above sea level. It is 2.2 miles (3.6 km) long and 1.2 miles (3.6km) wide. It is 5.8 miles (9.4km) around its base, and takes 3.5 hours to walk around.

The climb to the top is 1 mile (1.6kms), much of which is at a steep angle. The top is generally flat. The surface is made up of valleys, ridges, caves and weird shapes that were created through erosion over millions of years.

The local aboriginal Anangu people are the traditional owners of Uluru. They believe the rock has great spiritual powers.

HA LONG BAY

Vietnam — "where the dragon descends into the sea"

Located in the Quang Ninh province of Vietnam, Ha Long Bay is one incredible sight that runs along the coastline.

What makes it so amazing? The thousands of limestone islands and isles that are completely covered in jungle vegetation.

Ha Long means 'where the dragon descends into the sea' in Vietnamese.

The Vietnamese have a legend that the bay was created when a great mountain dragon charged towards the coast, its tail carving out valleys and crevasses. As the creature plunged into the sea, the area filled with water leaving only the tops of the islands visible.

Ha Long Bay was designated a World Heritage site in 1994.

The GREAT BLUE HOLE
Belize

"one of the top ten scuba diving sites in the world"

The Great Blue Hole is a giant sinkhole about 43 miles (70 km) off the coast of Belize.

The hole is shaped like a circle and is over 984 feet (300 meters) across and 407 feet (124 meters) deep.

The sinkhole was originally a limestone cave during the last glacial period, a time when sea levels were much lower. About 153,000 years ago, ocean levels began to rise and the cave system flooded. It eventually collapsed, creating a "vertical cave" in the ocean.

There are over 500 rare forms of animal and plant life that can only be located here.

In 2012 Discovery Channel ranked the Great Blue Hole as number one on its list of "The 10 Most Amazing Places on Earth".

SALAR DE UYUNI   Bolivia

"A Sea of Salt!"

At first glance it looks like a huge white ocean. Salar de Uyuni (or Salar de Tunupa) is the world's largest salt flat. The name originates from the Spanish word "Salar", meaning salt flat, and the Aymara word "Uyuni", meaning enclosure.

This salt flat is thought to contain over ten billion tons of salt.

It's the largest salt flat in the world and spans 4,086 square miles (10,582 square kilometers) in southwest Bolivia. As part of the Andes Mountains, it is located 11,995 feet (3,656 meters) above sea level.

The surface of the Salar de Uyuni is so flat that it only varies by 3 feet (less than 1 meter) in height over the entire salt flat.

Salar de Uyuni — BOLIVIA

The salt crust is about 10 feet (3 meters) thick. It is covered with a salt and water mix called brine, which is exceptionally rich in lithium.

The Salar contains large amounts of sodium, potassium, magnesium and lithium — 50% to 70% of the world's lithium reserves.

Scientists use the clear skies and the exceptional flatness of the surface to calibrate the altimeters of Earth's observation satellites.

The Salar de Uyuni is a major breeding ground for several species of flamingos.

The BLUE GROTTO
Capri, Italy

The Blue Grotto (Italian: Grotta Azzurra) is a sea cave on the coast of the island of Capri, southern Italy. Sunlight, passing through an underwater cavity and shining through the seawater, creates a blue reflection that lights up the grotto.

The cave is 200 feet (60 meters) long and 80 feet (25 meters) wide. If you place your hand underwater it will "glow" mysteriously thanks to the cave conditions and the light.

Entering the Blue Grotto lying flat

The cave mouth is 6.5 feet (2 meters) wide and roughly 3 feet (0.9 meter) high. You can only enter the grotto when tides are low and the sea is calm. To enter the grotto, visitors must lie flat on the bottom of a small rowboat.

During Roman times, the grotto was used as the personal swimming hole of Emperor Tiberius as well as a temple.

ARCHES NATIONAL PARK
Utah, USA

Arches National Park is a National Park in Eastern Utah, USA. It has over 2,000 natural stone arches, as well as hundreds of soaring pinnacles, massive fins, giant balanced rocks and other amazing rock formations.

Most of the formations at Arches National Park are made of soft red sandstone deposited 150 million years ago. The formations that we see today have been formed by millions of years of erosion and weathering.

To be classified as an arch, the opening must measure at least three feet (0.9 meter) across.

The largest arch in the park, Landscape Arch, spans 306 feet (93 meters) and is longer than a football field.

New arches are constantly forming, while old ones occasionally collapse. 23 arches have collapsed since 1977— most recently Wall Arch, collapsed in 2008.

The MATTERHORN

Switzerland and Italy

"the most photographed mountain in the world"

The Matterhorn is a mountain of the Alps, on the border between Switzerland and Italy. It is a huge and pyramid-shaped peak, with four steep sides or faces. It is 14,692 feet (4,478 meters) high, making it one of the highest summits in the Alps and Europe.

The Matterhorn is sometimes known as the "Mountain of Mountains" because of its beauty and difficulty to climb. Over time, the Matterhorn has become a symbol of the Swiss Alps and of the Alps in general.

The first successful climb of the Matterhorn was made in 1865 by a party led by Edward Whymper. However, this climb ended in disaster when 4 of the 7 climbing team members fell to their deaths on the descent.

The North face was not climbed until 1931. The West face, which is the highest of the four, was climbed only in 1962.

It is estimated that over 500 climbers have died on the Matterhorn since the first climb in 1865, making it one of the deadliest peaks in the world.

NGORANGORO CRATER

Tanzania, Africa

"Africa's Garden of Eden"

Ngorongoro Crater is the largest intact collapsed volcano in the world. It is shaped like a cooking pot. The crater is 100 square miles (259 square km) in area with walls 1960 feet (600 meters) in height.

It is believed that the Ngorongoro Crater volcano was originally taller than, or as high as Mount Kilimanjaro, one of the highest mountains in the world [approximately 16,000 feet (4,877 meters) high].

Ngorongoro Crater is found in Tanzania, Africa.

The Ngorongoro Crater is home to between 30,000 to 40,000 birds and animals, including pink flamingos and black rhino. The crater is also known as the 'Garden of Eden', due to its beauty and it being a paradise for animals.

In the centre of the Ngorongoro Crater is a salt-water lake.

THE GREAT BARRIER REEF
Australia
"biggest living thing seen from outer space"

The Great Barrier Reef is the only living thing that can be seen from outer space. The reef is the world's biggest single structure made by living organisms. The reef was built by billions of tiny organisms, known as coral polyps. The Great Barrier Reef is the world's largest reef system.

Over two million people visit each year. The Great Barrier Reef is composed of over 2,900 individual reefs. The Great Barrier Reef has over 900 islands stretching for over 1,610 miles (2,600 km).

The Great Barrier Reef is greater in size than the United Kingdom, Holland and Switzerland combined.

30 species of Whales, Dolphins, and Porpoises have been recorded in the Great Barrier Reef. 6 species of Turtles come to the reef to breed. 215 species of birds visit the reef to nest or roost on the islands. 17 species of Sea Snake live on the Great Barrier Reef. More than 1,500 fish species live on the reef.

Around 10 percent of the world's total fish species can be found within the Great Barrier Reef.

The Great Barrier Reef is very old, dating back as much as 20 million years.

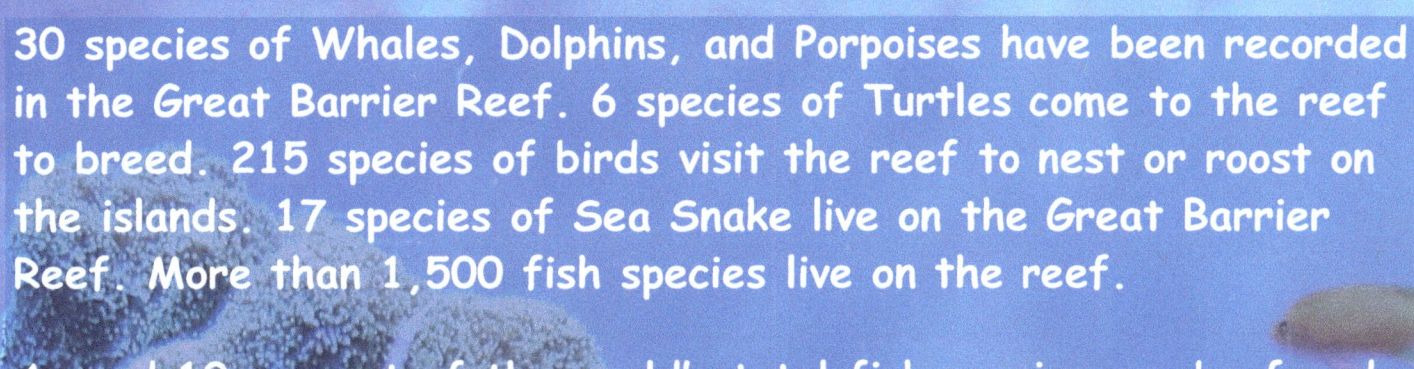

PANDO Utah, USA

"the Trembling Giant"

Pando means "I spread" in Latin. It is located in Fish Lake, Utah, USA.

Pando is a tree colony of thousands of trees that are actually a single organism. Belonging to the Quaking Aspen species of tree, Pando also has the nickname — "The Trembling Giant".

The Quaking Aspen is named for its leaves, which move easily in even a gentle breeze and produce a fluttering sound. When multiplied over the tens of thousands of trees Pando allows us to imagine a trembling giant.

Pando has one massive underground root system, which has been estimated at 80,000 years old. This would make it one of the oldest known living organisms on Earth.

Pando is also the heaviest living thing, at 13,000,000 pounds (6,000,00 kg).

It covers 106 acres (43 hectares), and has over 40,000 stems (trunks), which die individually and are replaced by new stems growing from its roots.

The average age of Pando's stems is 130 years old, as measured by tree rings.

IGUAZU FALLS
Brazil, South America

One of the great natural wonders of the world, Iguazu Falls is found on the border between Brazil and Argentina. The waterfall system consists of 275 falls along the Iguazu River.

Iguazu means "big water" in native Guarani Indian language.

Most of the falls are about 210 feet (64 meters) high. The most impressive of them all is called the Devil's Throat — a U-shaped, 269 feet (82 meter) high, 492 feet (150 meter) wide and 2300 feet (700 meter) long waterfall.

Iguazu Falls is nearly twice as tall as Niagara Falls. It is nearly 3 times wider than Niagara Falls and significantly wider than the Victoria Falls.

The amount of water pouring from these falls to the Iguazu River is equally amazing.

Depending on the time of the year, the rate of water flow can be as much as 4,953,226 gallons (18,750,000 liters) per second - enough to fill 5 Olympic swimming pools in 1 second.

THE GRAND CANYON
Arizona, USA

The Grand Canyon is a steep-sided canyon carved by the Colorado River. It is found in the state of Arizona in the USA. The canyon is 277 miles (446 km) long, up to 18 miles (29 km) wide and reaches a depth of 6,093 feet (1,857 meters).

The Canyon is known as one of the "7 Natural Wonders of the World".

5 million people visit the Grand Canyon each year.

The Grand Canyon took between 3—6 million years to form.

It was formed by the Colorado River, which flows west through the canyon and averages about 300 feet (91 meters) wide, 100 feet (30 meters) in depth and flows at an average speed of 4 miles per hour (6.5 km per hour).

Even today the Colorado River continues to erode the canyon and alter its shape.

The Grand Canyon includes 70 different species of mammals, 250 species of birds, 25 types of reptiles and 5 species of amphibians.

The Grand Canyon has many layers of rock and soil. The striped colors you see come from the minerals in the rock. The shades of these include red, orange, yellow, white, and even the color purple.

Each layer of rock — known as a stratum — is a different rock group which was formed at different points in time. The top layer of rock is Kaibab Limestone. It is some 240 million years old. The bottom layer is called the Vishnu Schist. It is estimated to be about 1.7 billion years old.

THE GIANT'S CAUSEWAY

Northern Ireland

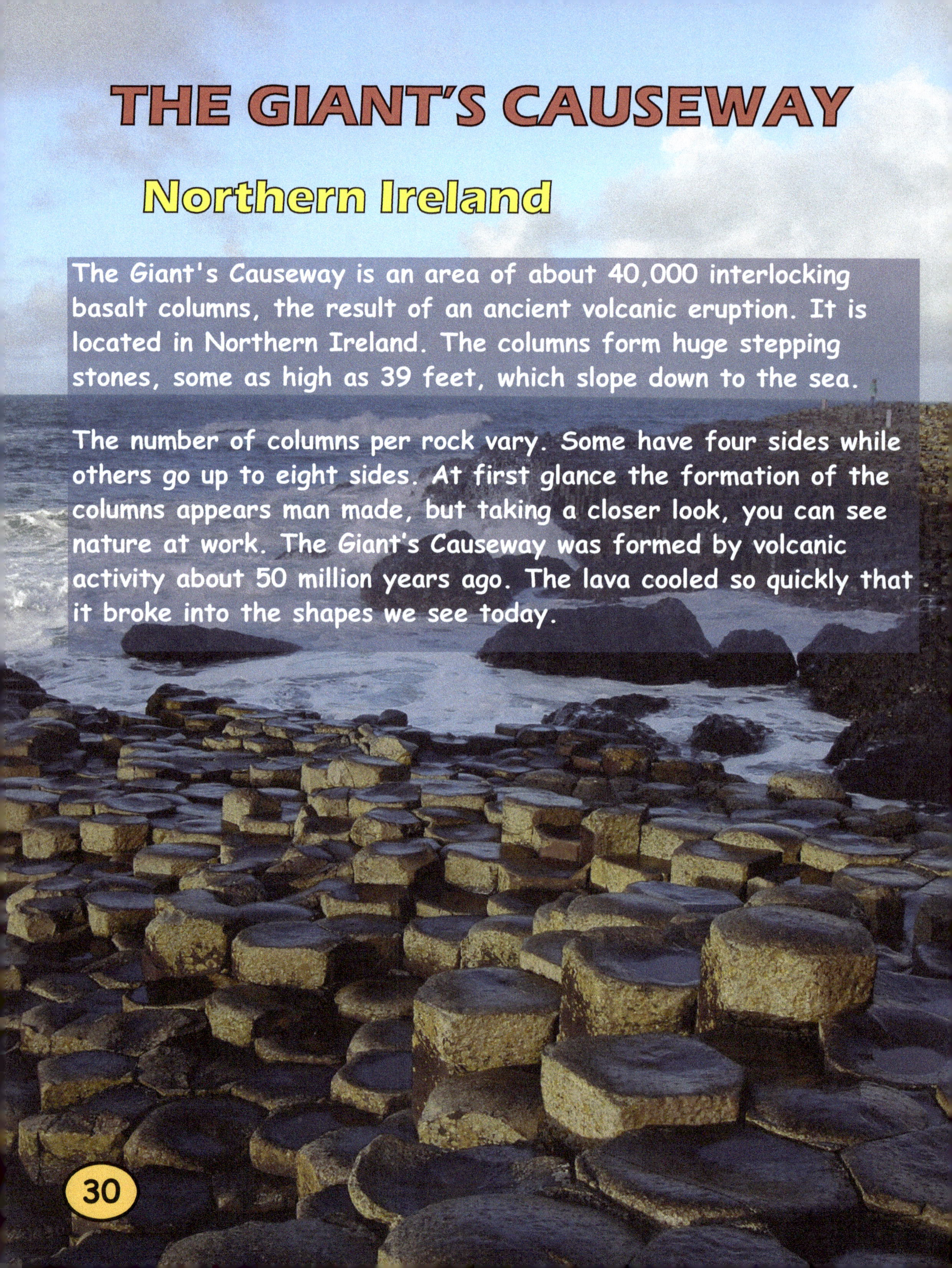

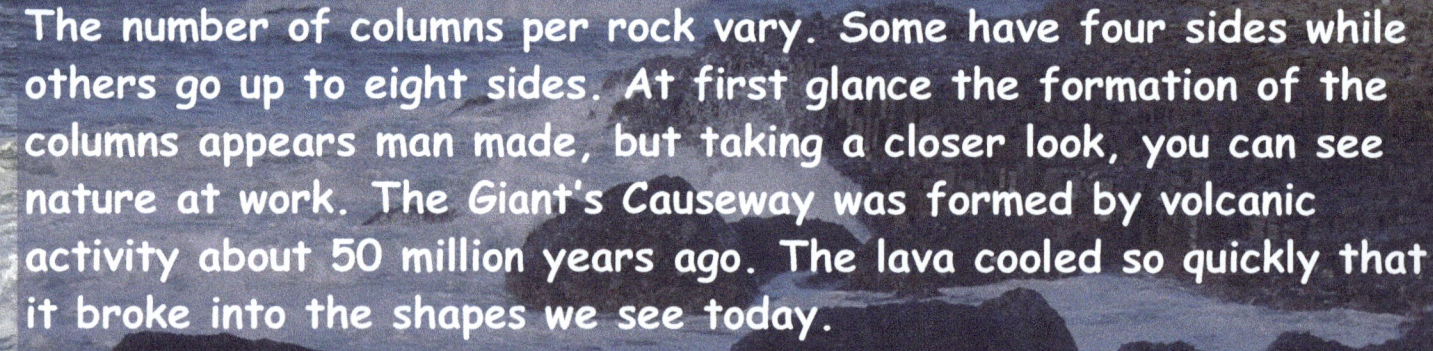

The Giant's Causeway is an area of about 40,000 interlocking basalt columns, the result of an ancient volcanic eruption. It is located in Northern Ireland. The columns form huge stepping stones, some as high as 39 feet, which slope down to the sea.

The number of columns per rock vary. Some have four sides while others go up to eight sides. At first glance the formation of the columns appears man made, but taking a closer look, you can see nature at work. The Giant's Causeway was formed by volcanic activity about 50 million years ago. The lava cooled so quickly that it broke into the shapes we see today.

Many of the columns fit together so closely that it is impossible to insert a knife blade between them.

A local legend says that the Giant's Causeway was built by Finn McCool, a magical giant. Finn supposedly built the causeway so that he could reach Scotland without getting his feet wet.

The rocky coastline around the Giant's Causeway has caused many shipwrecks.

YUKI-NO-OTANI SNOW CANYON

Honshu, Japan

The Tateyama Murodo Plain on the Japanese island of Honshu receives some of the heaviest snowfalls in the world every year.

It is at an altitude of 8,000 feet (2,438 meters) above sea level.

Each year at the beginning of Spring a huge snow wall called the Yuki-no-Otani Snow Canyon is formed to open up the road through the Tateyama Murodo Plain.

The 1,650 feet (502 meter) long snow wall is formed each Spring on either side of the highway after snow is cleared.

Often the snow walls on both sides of the road reach 66 feet (20 meters) in height, close to the height of a 7 story building.

One side of the road is left open for pedestrians to walk.

The walls are still 33 feet (10 meters) high even in late June at the end of Spring.

THANKS FOR READING!

Please leave a review at the website where you bought this book and tell others what you liked about it.

Visit www.TJRob.com for a FREE eBook and to see TJ Rob's other exciting books

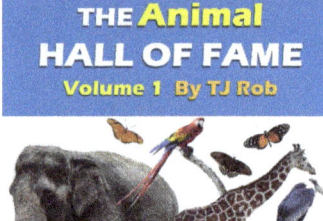

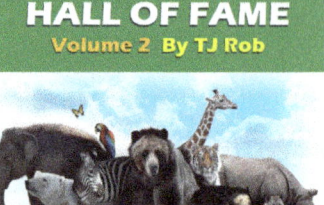
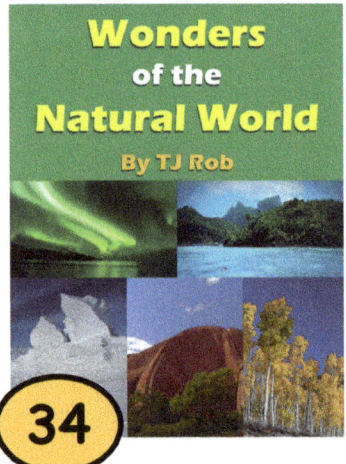
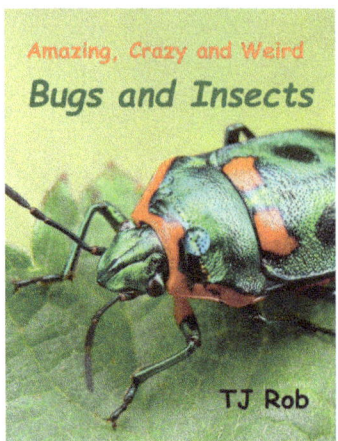

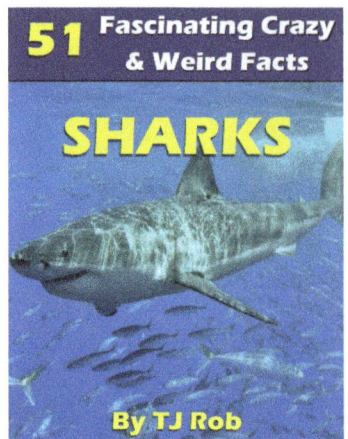

www.ingramcontent.com/pod-product-compliance
Lightning Source LLC
Chambersburg PA
CBHW040005080526
44586CB00027B/2893